CHARLES MINGUS
EASY PIANO SOLOS

ISBN 978-1-4234-2643-1

HAL•LEONARD®
CORPORATION

7777 W. BLUEMOUND RD. P.O. BOX 13819 MILWAUKEE, WI 53213

In Australia Contact:
Hal Leonard Australia Pty. Ltd.
4 Lentara Court
Cheltenham, Victoria, 3192 Australia
Email: ausadmin@halleonard.com.au

Visit Hal Leonard Online at
www.halleonard.com

BETTER GET HIT IN YOUR SOUL

By CHARLES MINGUS

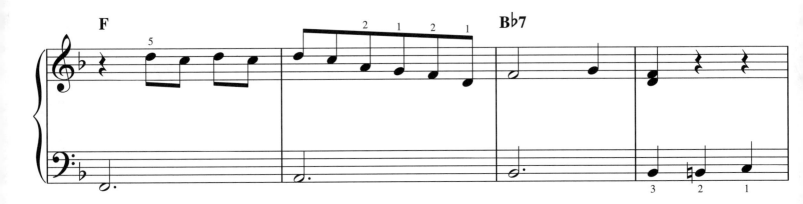

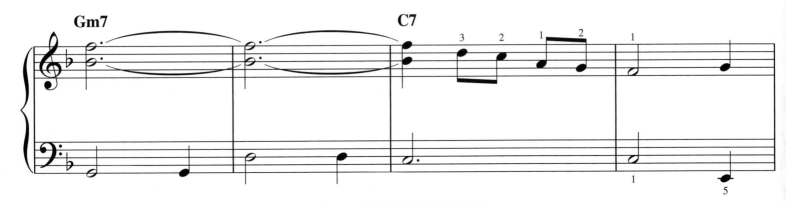

4

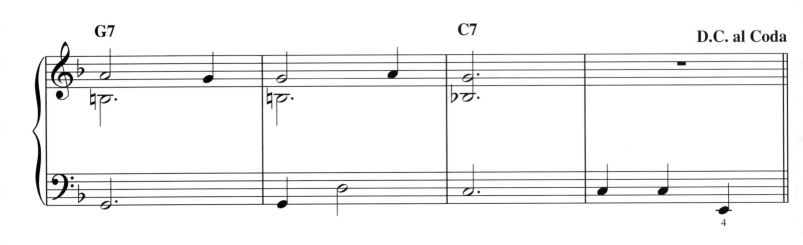

D.C. al Coda

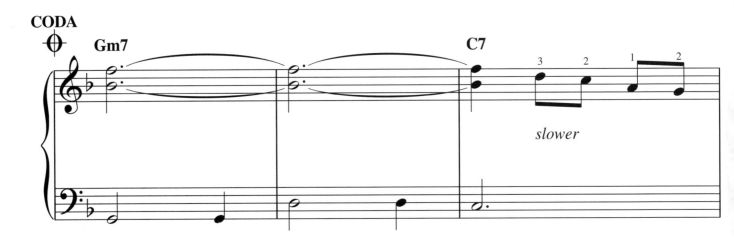

CODA

slower

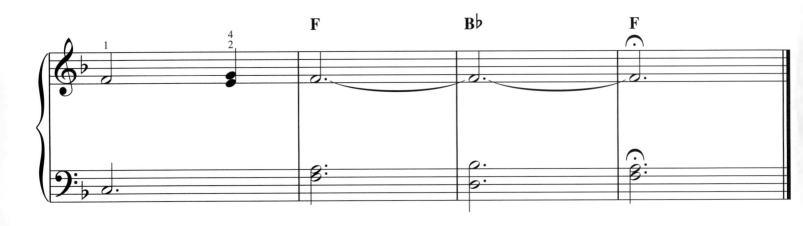

BOOGIE STOP SHUFFLE

By CHARLES MINGUS

Up-tempo Swing

6

CELIA

By CHARLES MINGUS

Moderately, in 2

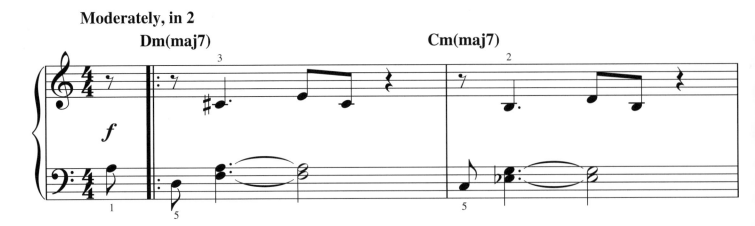

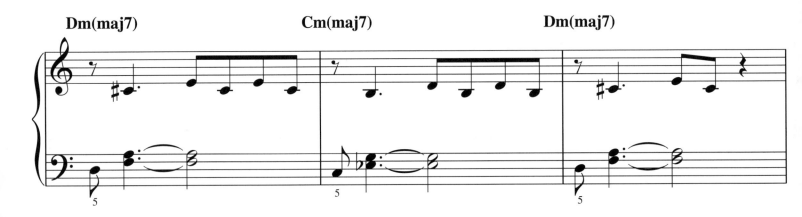

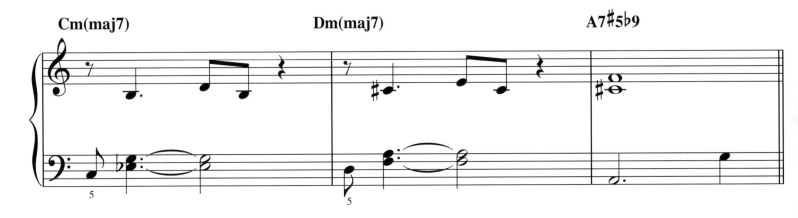

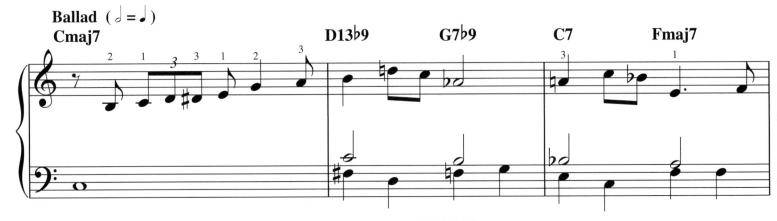

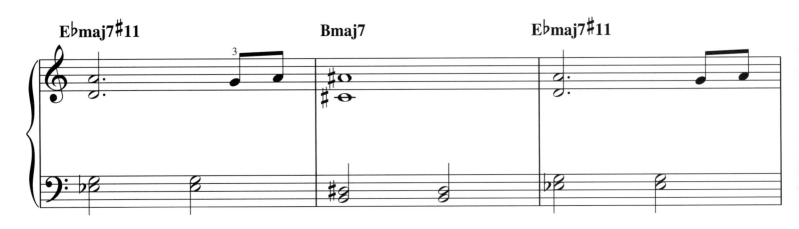

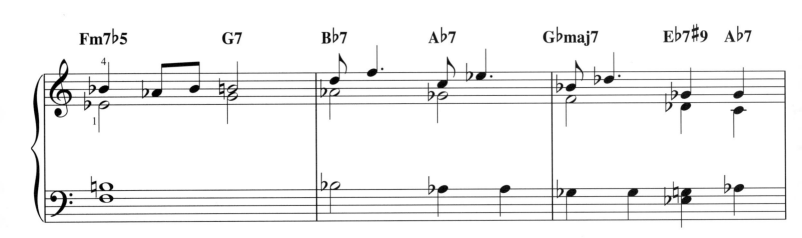

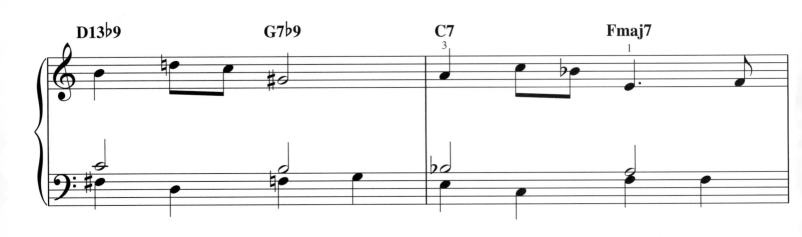

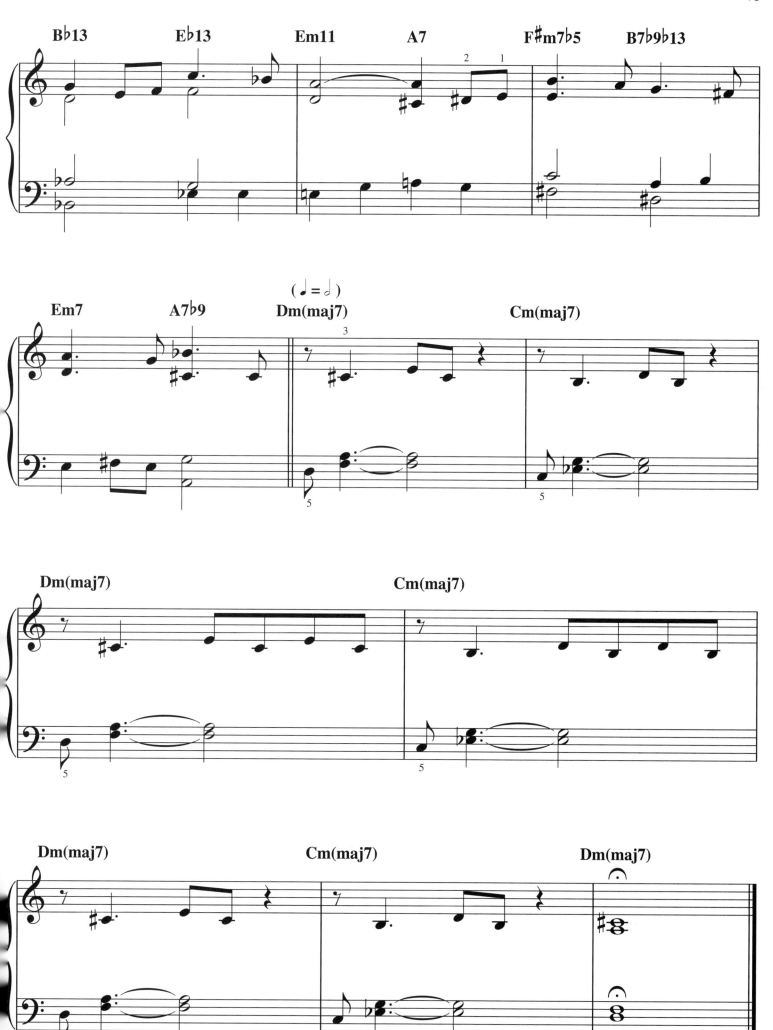

CHAIR IN THE SKY

Words by JONI MITCHELL
Music by CHARLES MINGUS

DIANE
(Alice's Wonderland)

By CHARLES MINGUS

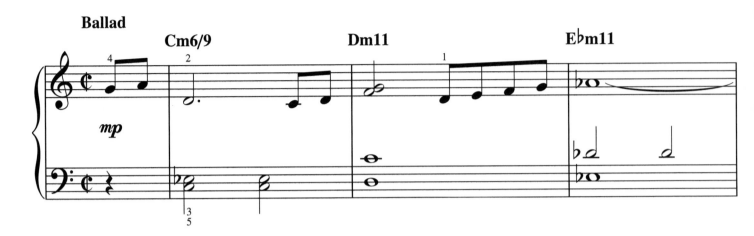

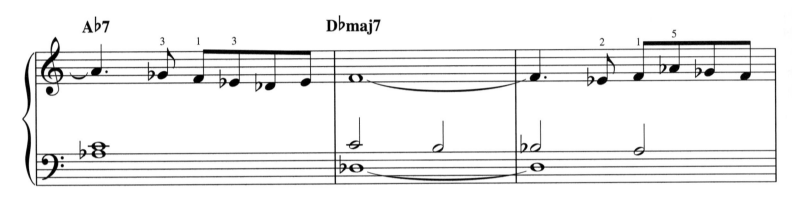

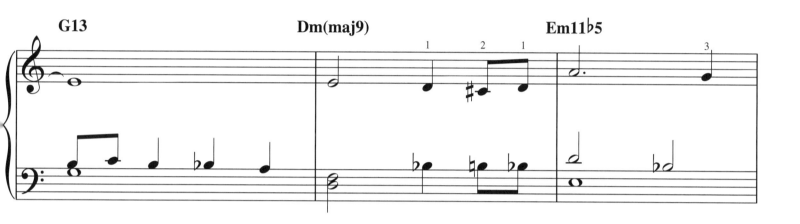

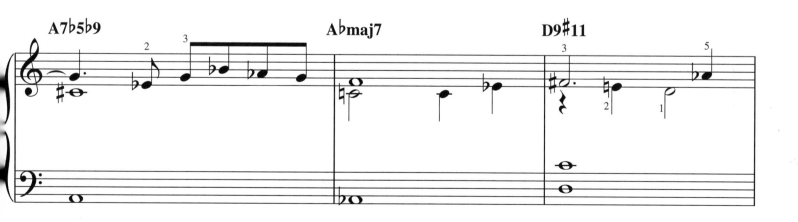

18

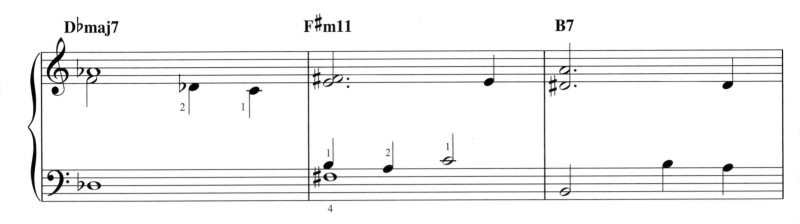

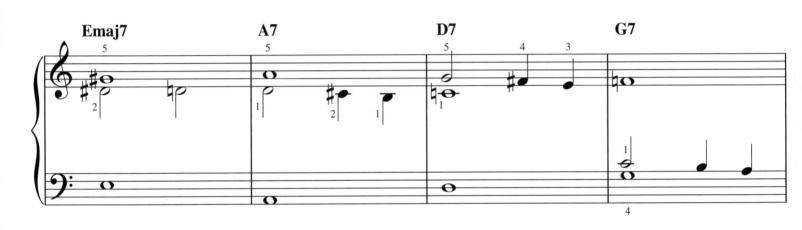

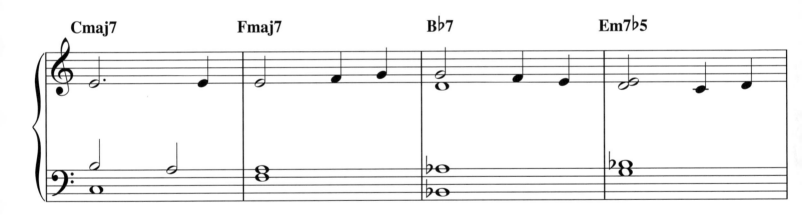

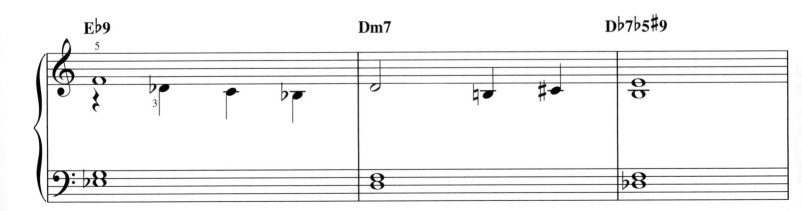

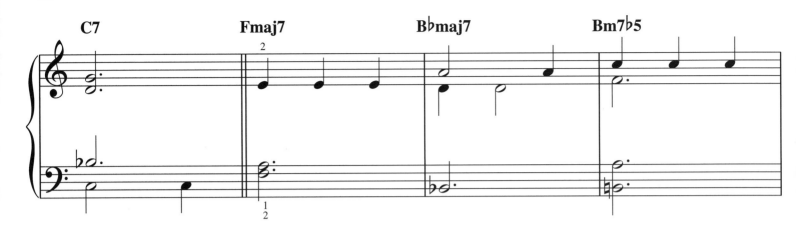

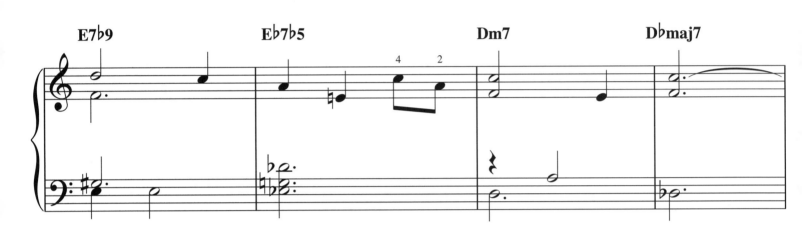

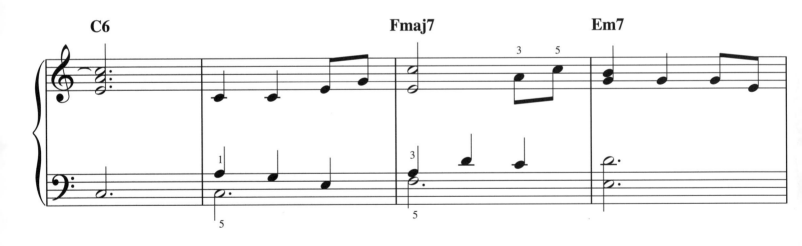

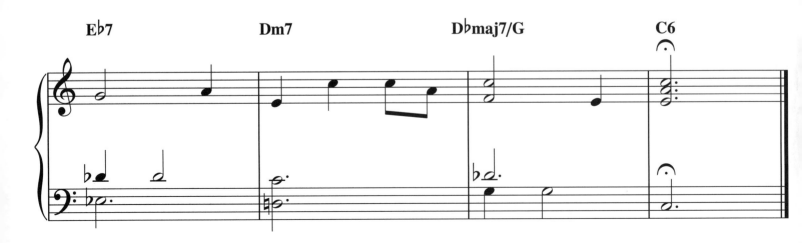

DUKE ELLINGTON'S SOUND OF LOVE

Words and Music by
CHARLES MINGUS

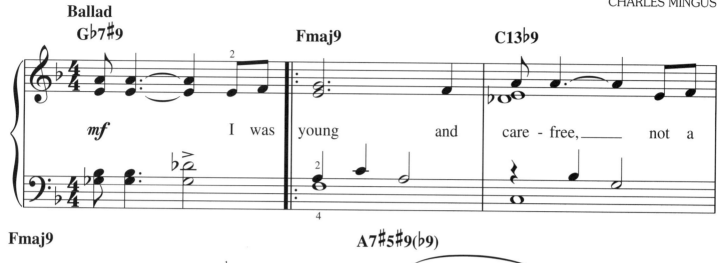

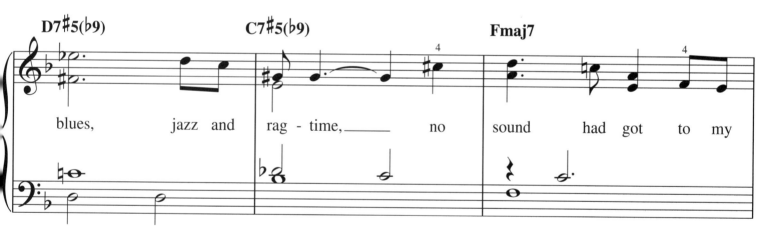

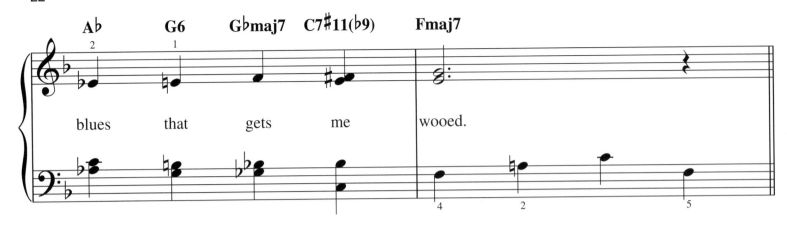

Ab G6 Gbmaj7 C7#11(b9) Fmaj7

blues   that   gets   me   wooed.

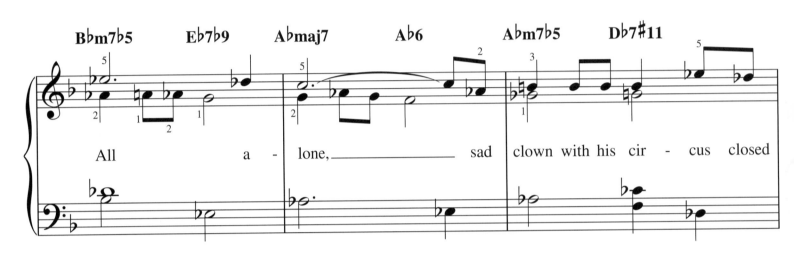

Bbm7b5   Eb7b9   Abmaj7   Ab6   Abm7b5   Db7#11

All   a - lone,_____ sad   clown with his cir - cus closed

Gbmaj7   F#m7   B7   Emaj7

down.   Lost   on my mer - ry - go - round   came a mel - o -

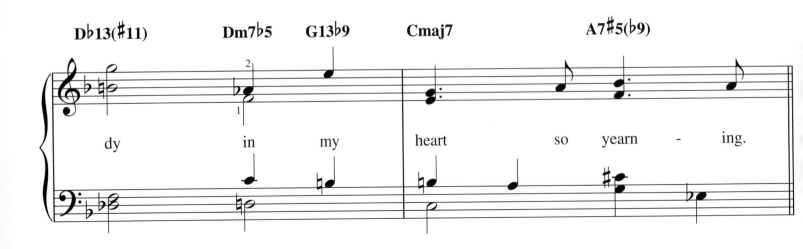

Db13(#11)   Dm7b5   G13b9   Cmaj7   A7#5(b9)

dy   in   my   heart   so   yearn - ing.

Taught me to hear mu - sic out of love, from the

soul, for this life we all live in - fi -

nite with the lov - er and be - lov - ed,_____ as

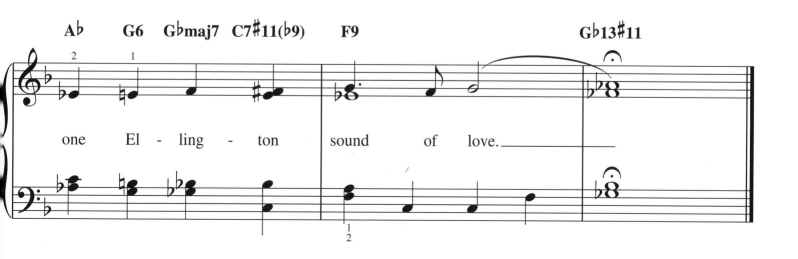

one El - ling - ton sound of love._____

GOODBYE PORK PIE HAT

By CHARLES MINGUS

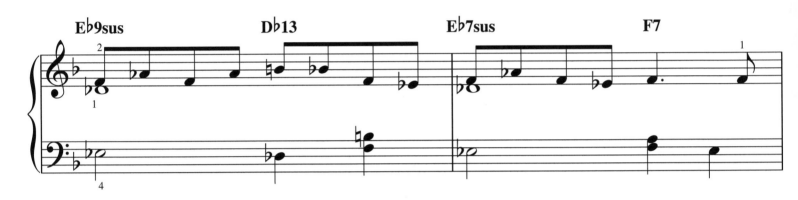

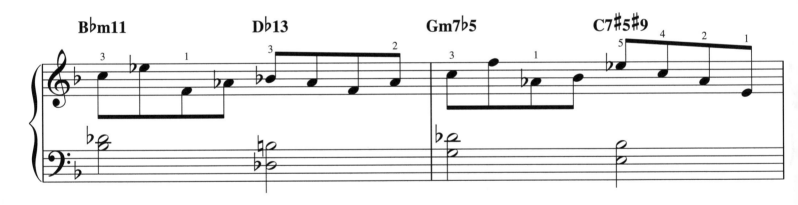

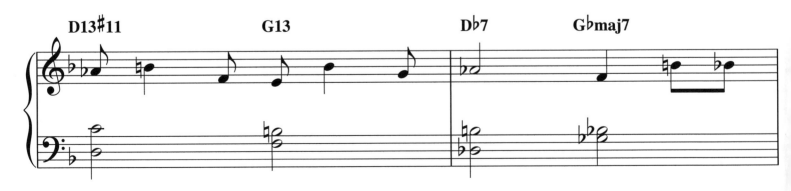

HORA DECUBITUS

By CHARLES MINGUS

Up-tempo Swing

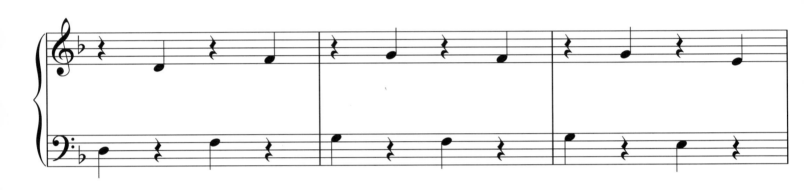

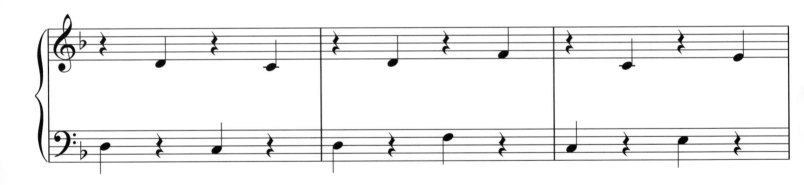

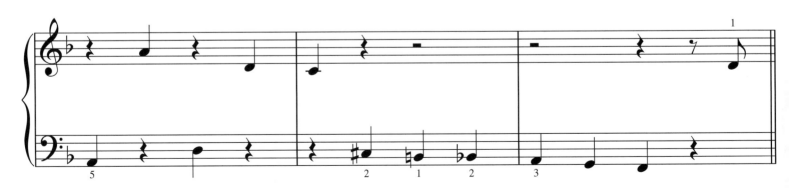

28

JELLY ROLL

By CHARLES MINGUS

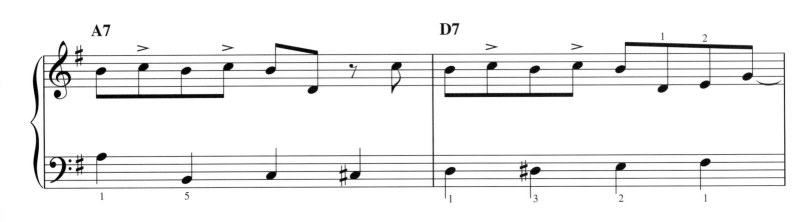

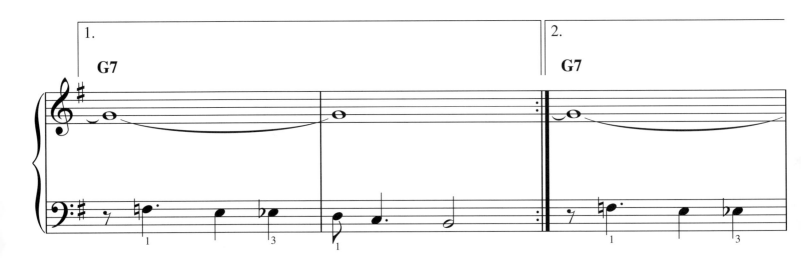

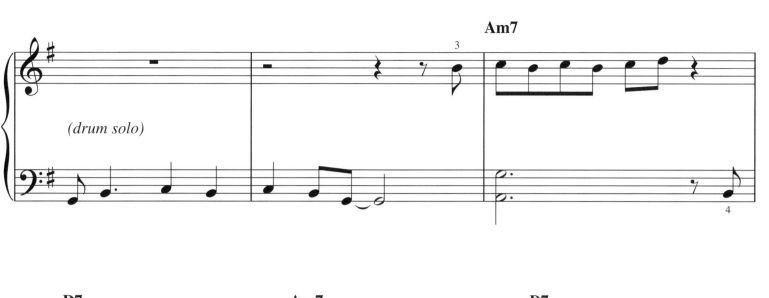

(drum solo)

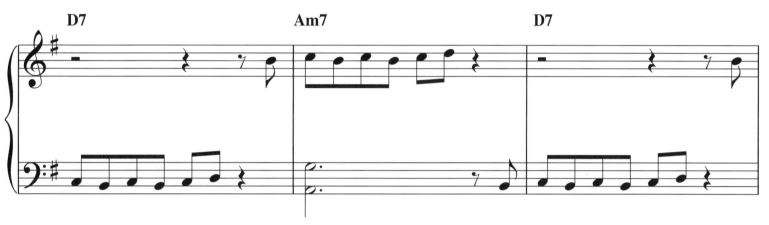

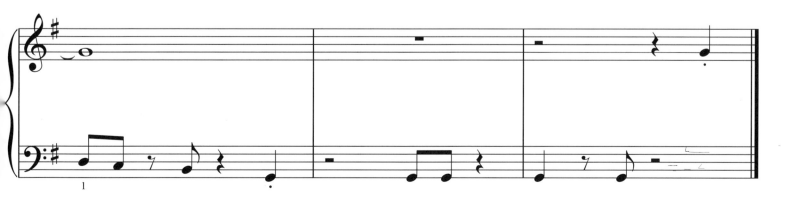

INVISIBLE LADY

By CHARLES MINGUS

Ballad, with half-time feel

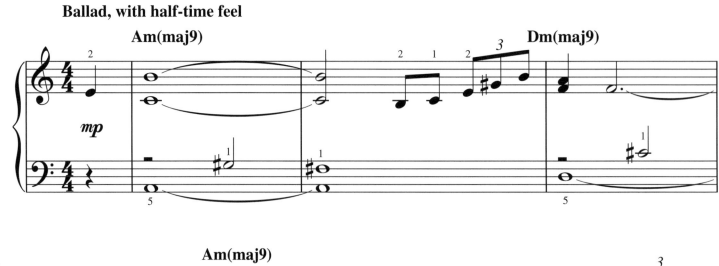

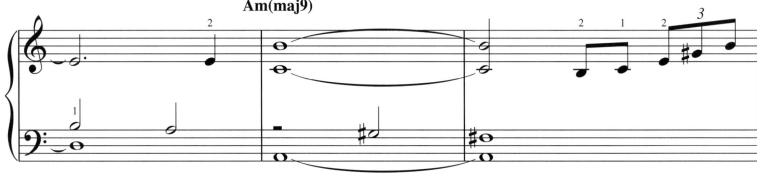

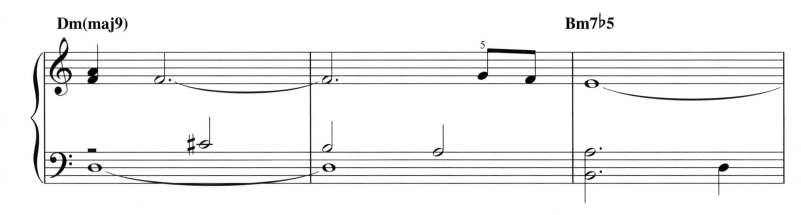

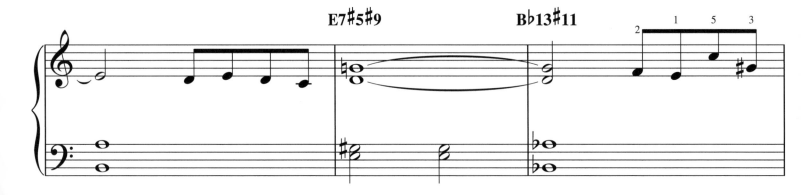

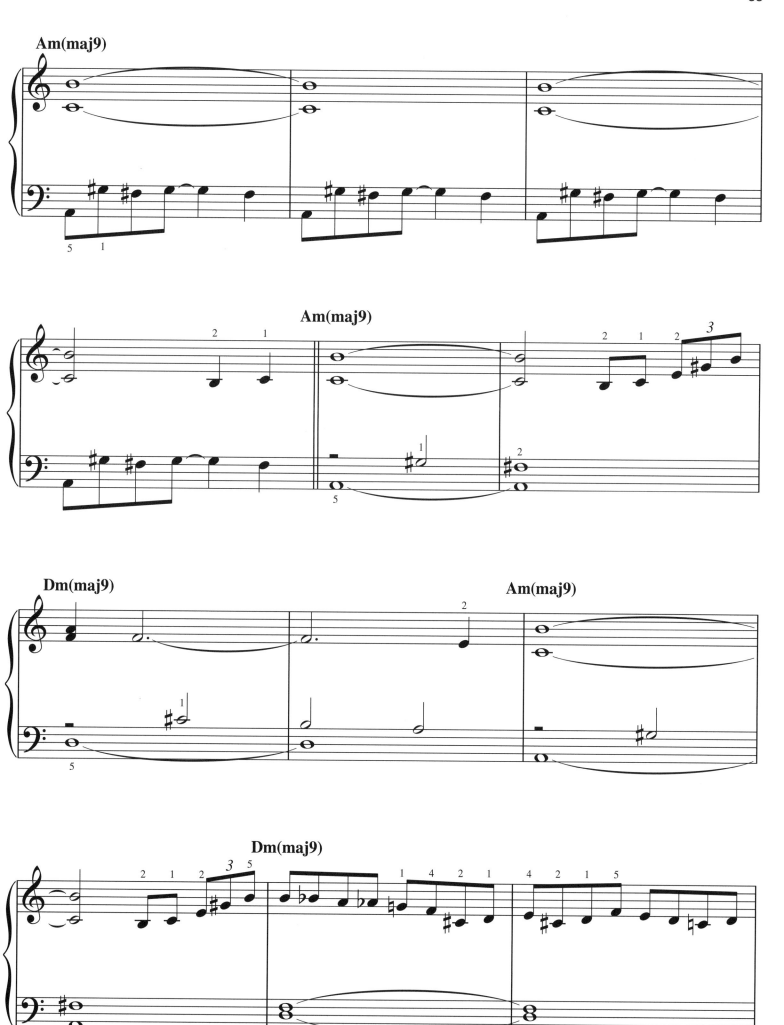

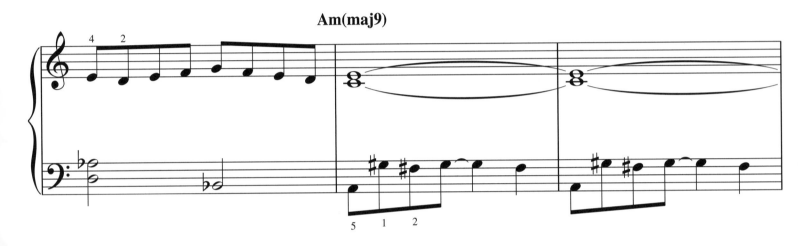

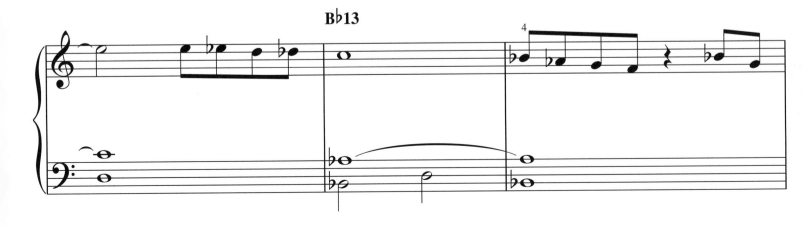

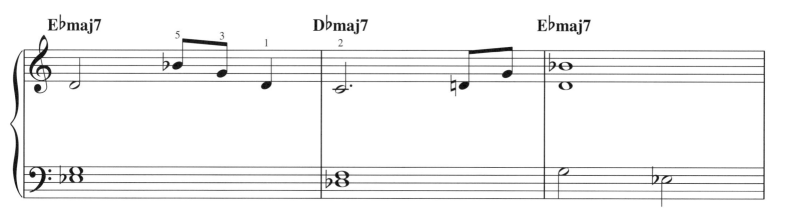

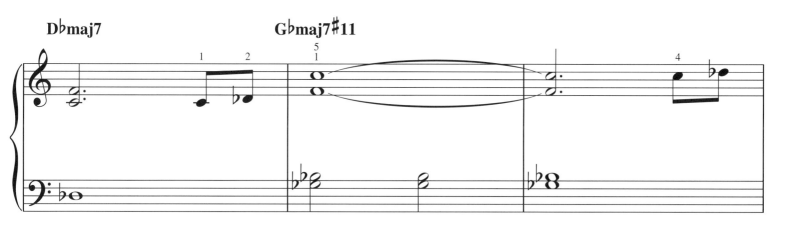

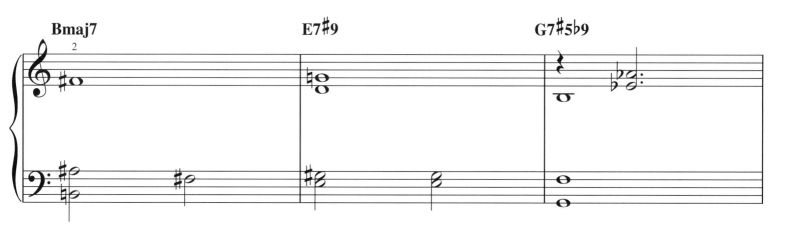

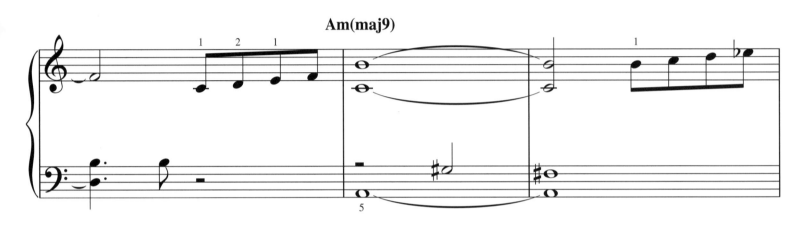

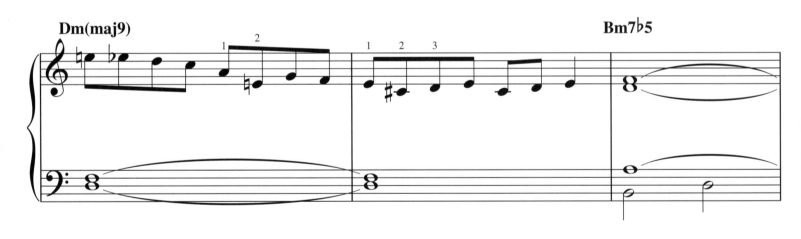

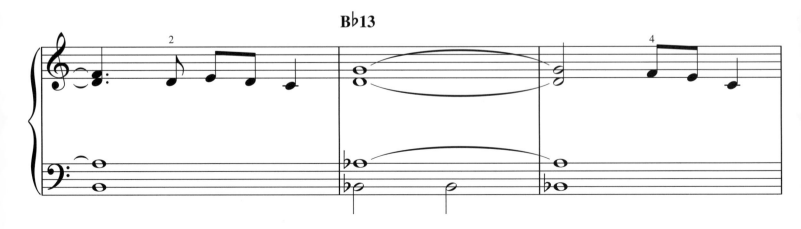

Am(maj9)

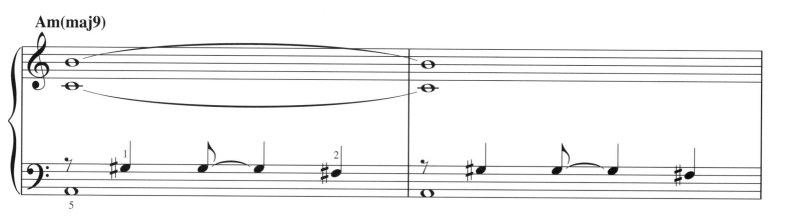

ad lib.

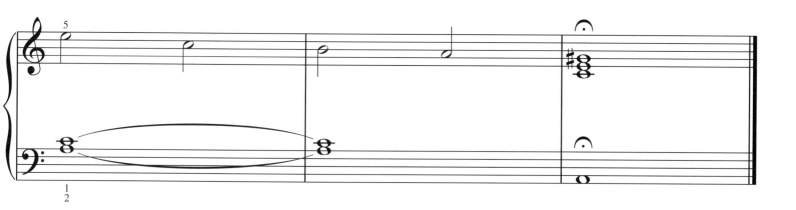

NODDIN' YA HEAD BLUES

By CHARLES MINGUS

Slow Swing

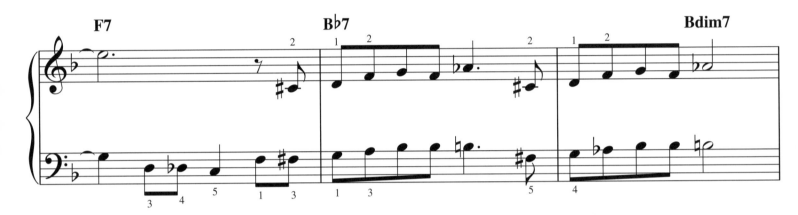

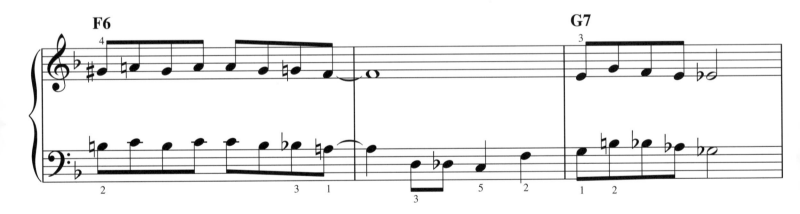

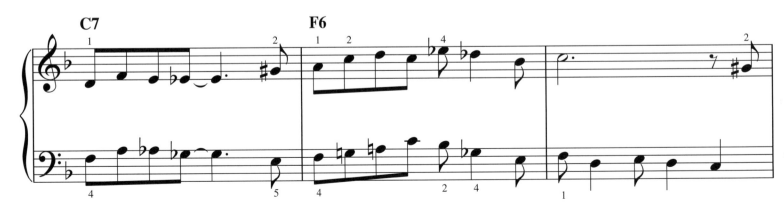

NOSTALGIA IN TIMES SQUARE

By CHARLES MINGUS

42

PEGGY'S BLUE SKYLIGHT

By CHARLES MINGUS

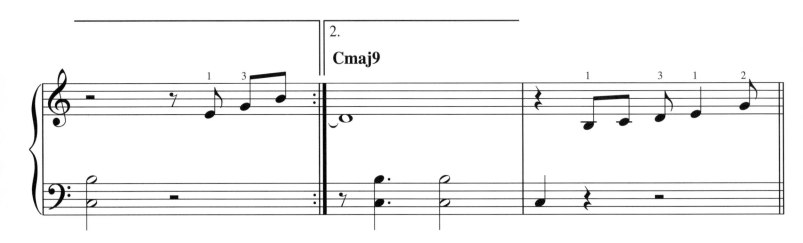

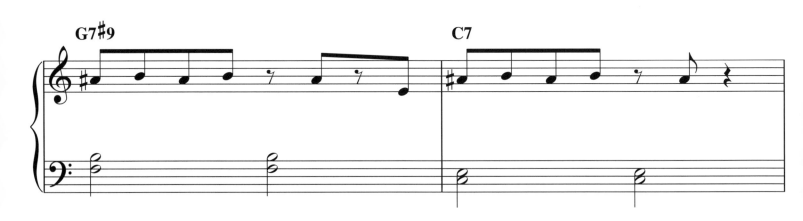

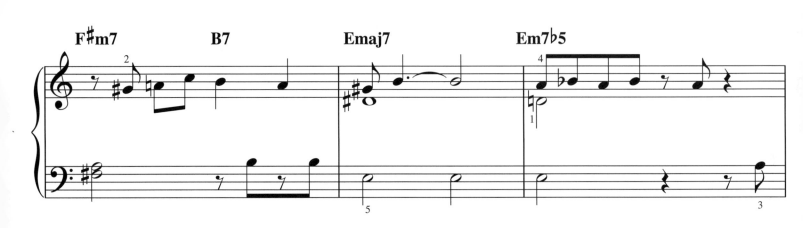

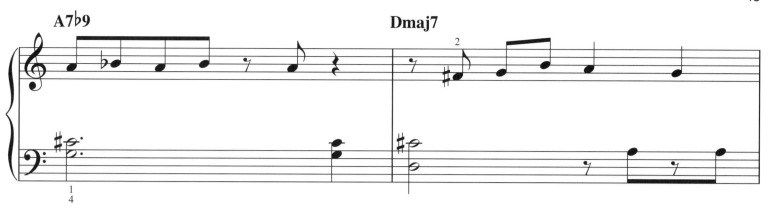

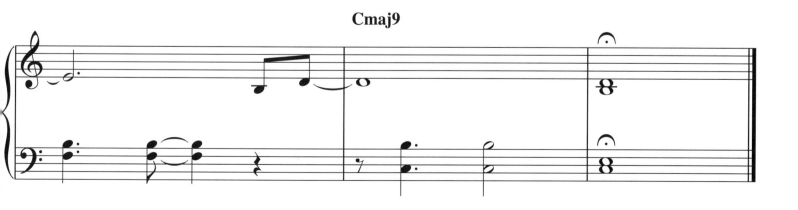

PORTRAIT

Words and Music by
CHARLES MINGUS

Ballad, with a half-time feel

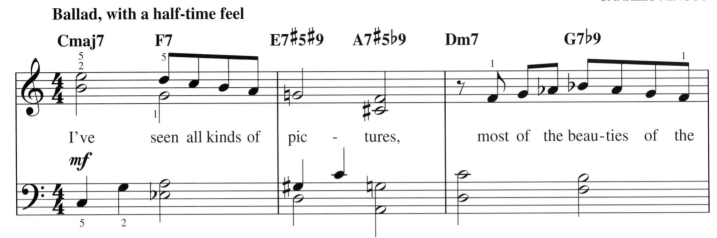

I've seen all kinds of pic - tures, most of the beau - ties of the

world, from plac - es I've trav - eled I still re - call this

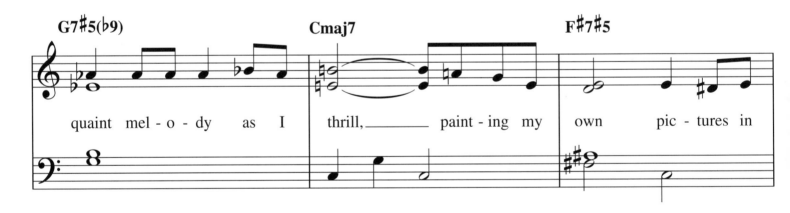

quaint mel - o - dy as I thrill,_____ paint - ing my own pic - tures in

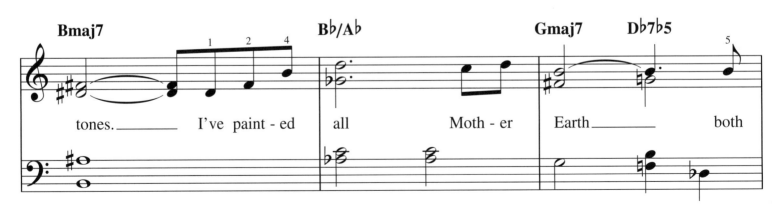

tones._____ I've paint - ed all Moth - er Earth_____ both

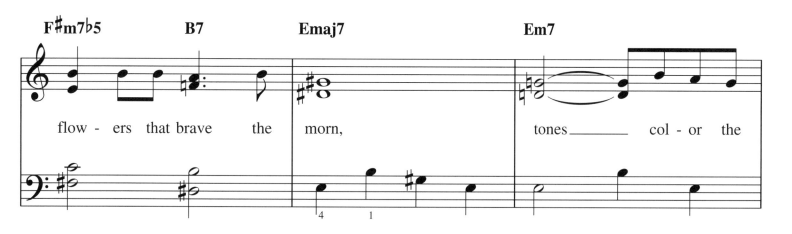

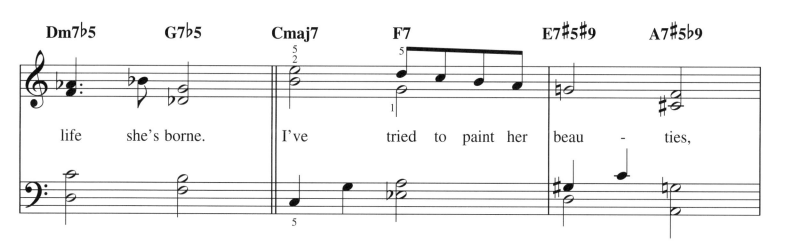

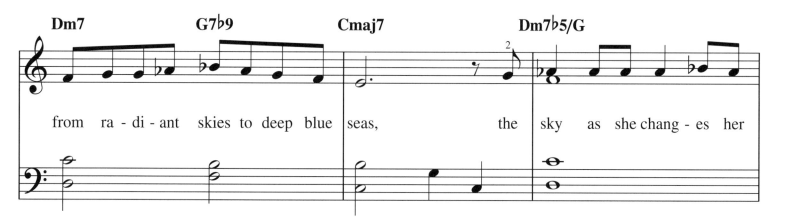

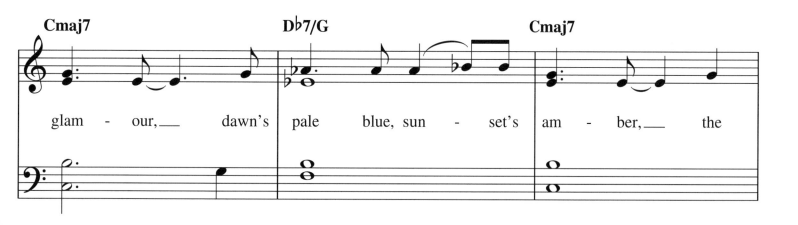

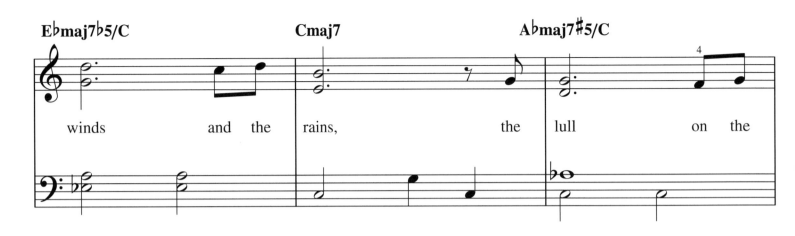

winds and the rains, the lull on the

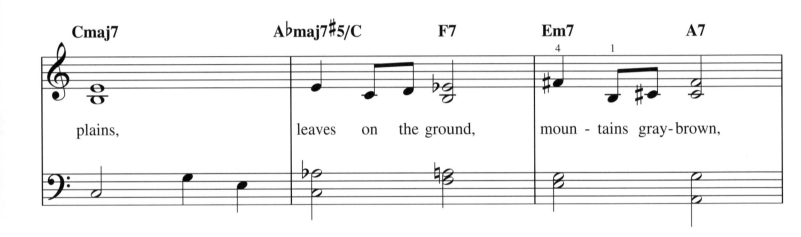

plains, leaves on the ground, moun - tains gray - brown,

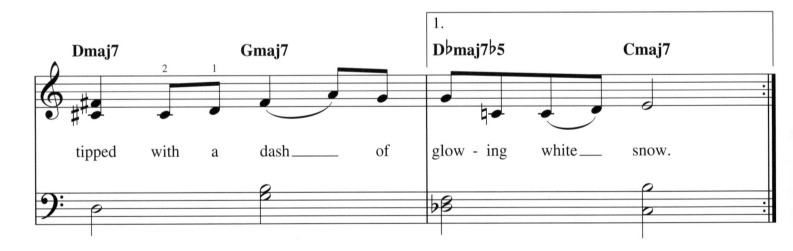

1.

tipped with a dash_____ of glow - ing white____ snow.

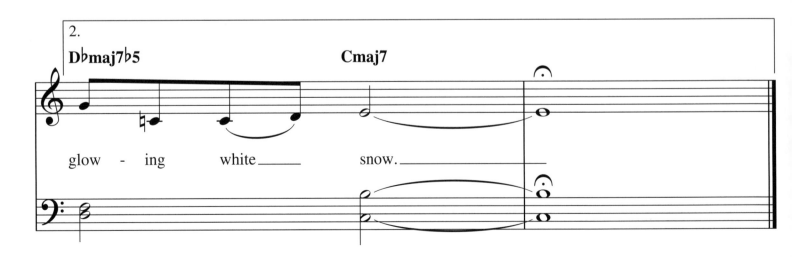

2.

glow - ing white_____ snow._____

SONG WITH ORANGE

By CHARLES MINGUS

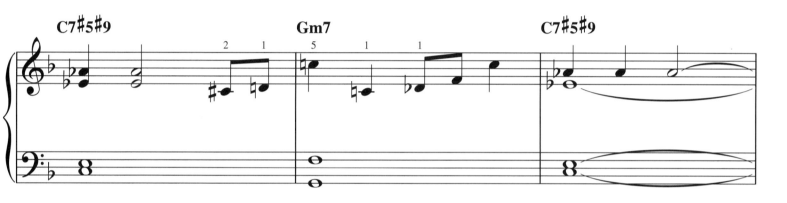

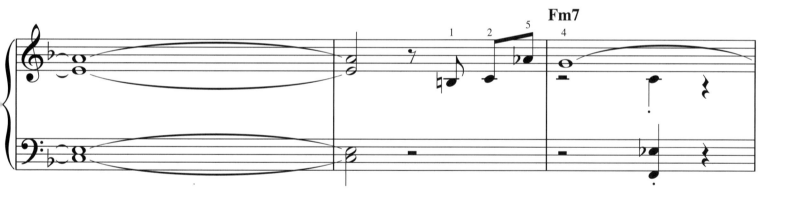

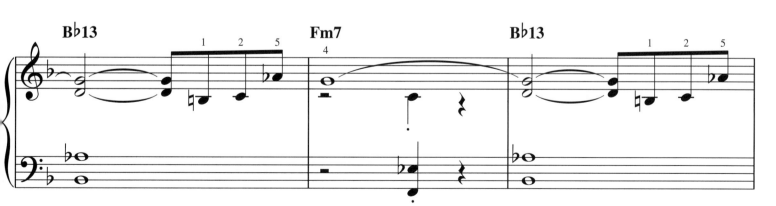

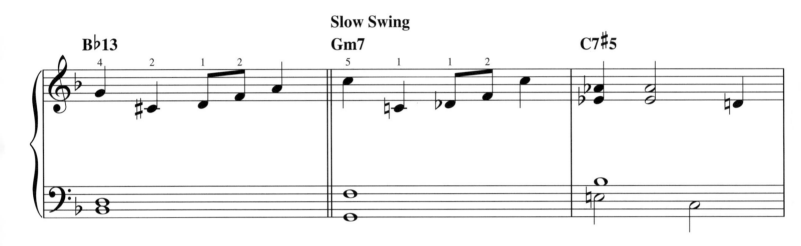

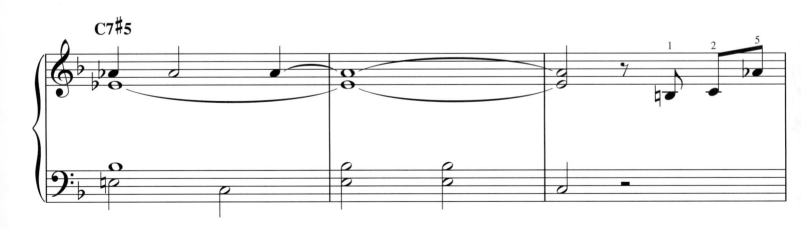

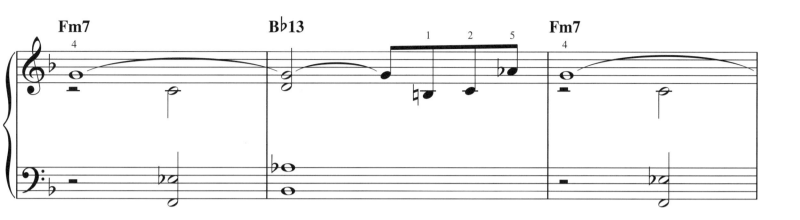

SUE'S CHANGES

By CHARLES MINGUS

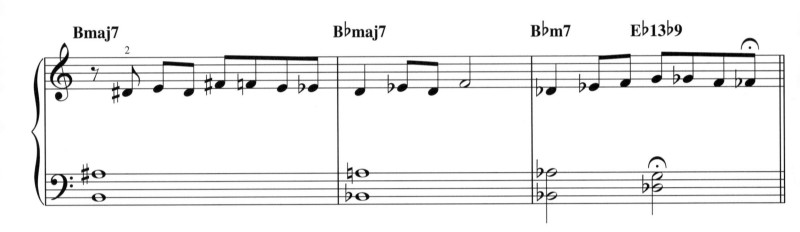

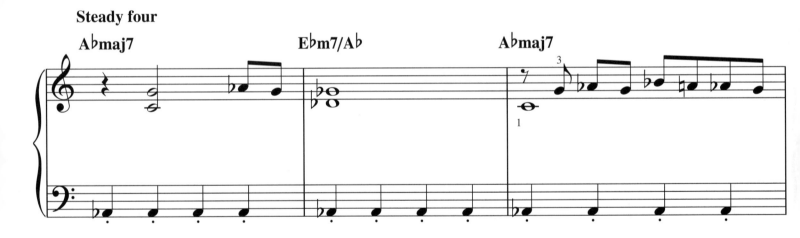

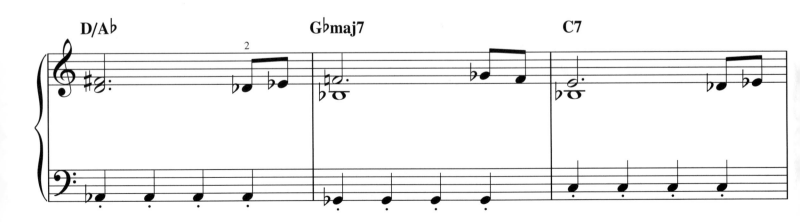

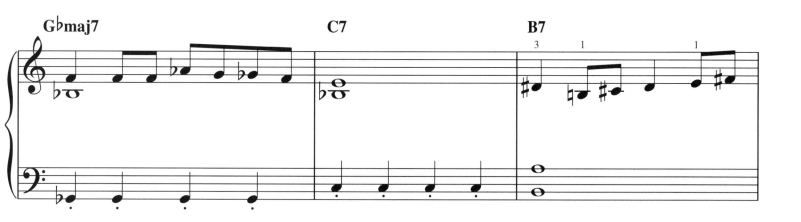

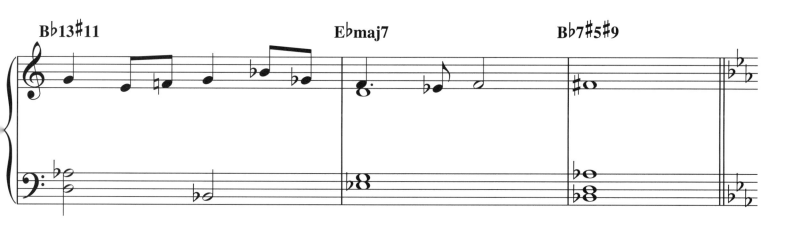

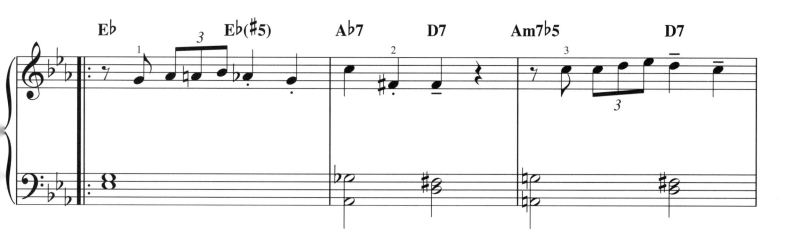

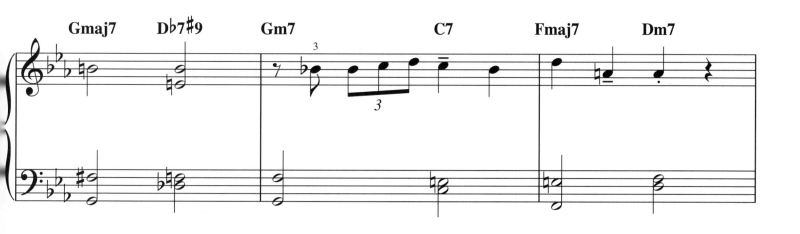

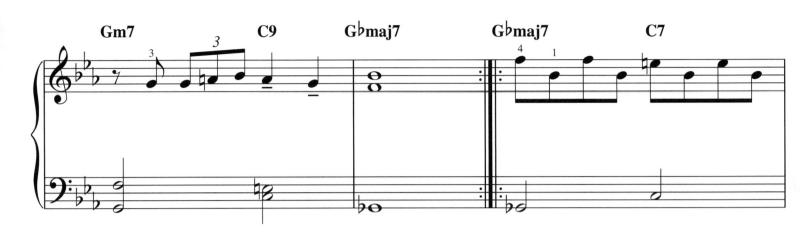

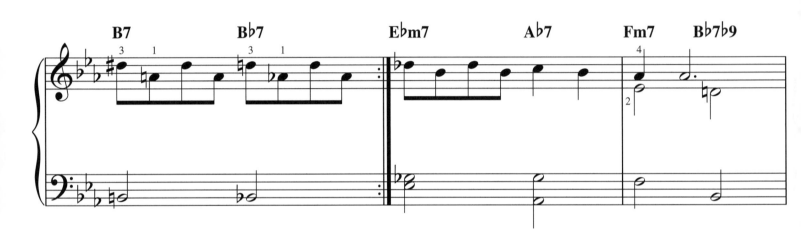

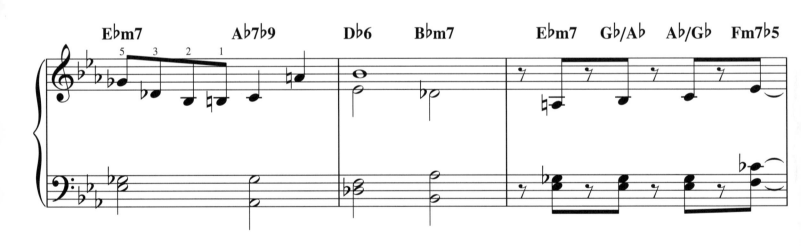

SWEET SUCKER DANCE

Words by JONI MITCHELL
Music by CHARLES MINGUS

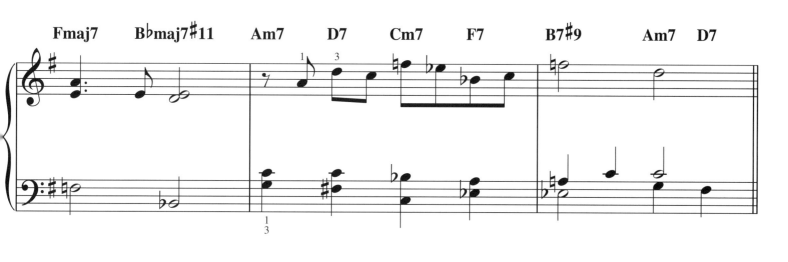

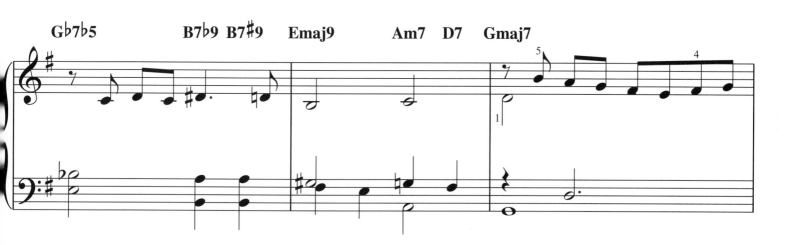

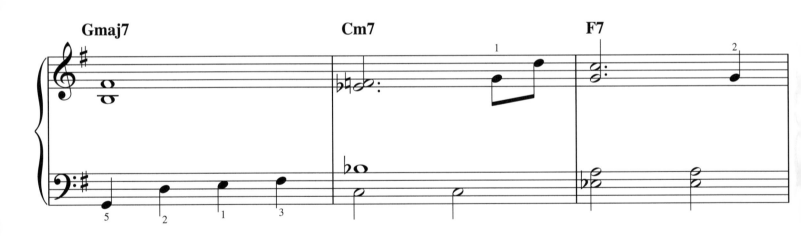